Over
600 Icebreakers
& Games

-

team building games & questions

for teams

and small groups

compiled & edited by

Jennifer Carter

DEDICATION

With heartfelt thanks to memorable small group leaders over the years, Ivor & Mary, Kevin & Lorna, Pete & Deborah. You have enriched my life, lifted me up when I was down, inspired me and encouraged me.

Thanks to all those in my own small group - we're a great bunch of oddballs that only someone with a sense of humor could have put together. Each one of you has a special place in my heart.

I am so thankful to God for each of you and our times of laughter and tears together.

TABLE OF CONTENTS

INTRODUCTION

This book contains over six hundred icebreaker questions directed primarily towards small groups and teams. It offers a selection of team-building games and activities.

Everyone thinks it's easy to think up an icebreaker or game – until it's their turn to think one up!

This book was written for anyone who wants to use icebreaker questions or team games. It is a simple resource that supplies everything you need in one place.

On these pages, you'll find hundreds of icebreakers organized into fourteen different "themes." The themes range from some simple get-to–know-you questions to more searching questions that explore feelings, learning, beliefs and thinking outside the box.

This book was created for busy people. It is laid out in a manner which allows you to dip in and find just what you need. In less than sixty seconds, you can find an icebreaker question or team game to use.

The first chapters cover why icebreakers are so valuable and how to make best use of them with your team or small group.

Then we move to the icebreaker questions themselves, each chapter with a different theme.

Finally, there are a many teambuilding games and activities for occasions when you want to ring the changes.

Once word gets out that you've got this book, with its short-cut to energizing your team, people will be begging to borrow it!

WHY ICEBREAKERS?
BREAKING BARRIERS & BUILDING TEAM

What Is An Icebreaker?

An icebreaker can take the form of questions, games or activities. It can be funny or serious, helping the group to get to know each other better, one small step at a time.

Using Icebreaker Questions & Games

Using icebreaker questions and games can be a fun activity at informal get-togethers, team meetings, parties and socials.

An icebreaker can help people discover the things they have in common, their shared experiences and their similar (and different) hopes.

Some of these icebreakers encourage more intimacy than others. They explore feelings, values and dreams, while others are simply fun!

It's healthy for your small group to regularly welcome new members, and icebreakers are the perfect tool to help guests feel at ease and get to know the group better.

Breaking Down Barriers

Icebreakers can help your meeting to get off to a great start, and they also make it easier for individuals to relax and feel more comfortable with people they don't know.

Over a period of time, icebreakers and teambuilding games can help people get to know each other. They encourage interaction and act as catalysts to help people more deeply understanding of one another.

Icebreakers have the power to transform and rejuvenate your team, so don't undervalue them.

Building Bridges

Small groups are places where real community can take place. In a team setting, friendships are built, individuals are encouraged and genuine community is built.

In today's society, people from very different backgrounds are often called to work together as a team. While the team may not naturally have much in common, a good team leader wants to build the unity and strength of their team.

Building Success

If you look at the business model for some of the most successful companies in the world, you'll discover one thing that they have in common: great teams.

Successful businesses invest time in *building great teams*. For example, Zappos focuses on "building positive team and family spirit." Apple uses teams to forge ahead with innovation.

Being in a small group or on a team gives individuals the opportunity to feel like they are a part of something greater than themselves. They have the opportunity to share their feelings and thoughts, to understand and implement the values of the organization or team and to get committed to the collective vision.

Small groups and teams can also be one of the key places where people engage in meaningful friendship.

The Value of Icebreakers - An Example

One group recently did an impromptu icebreaker. The question posed was a fun one: "If you were a chocolate cake, how would you be decorated?"

The answers were as diverse as the individuals within the group.

Some showed incredible creativity, describing a delicious frosting and elaborate cake decorations. Others were methodical in their descriptions of chopping up a chocolate bar for decoration.

Everybody took part, and each person was valued for their contribution. Everyone learned a little more about the others' likes and dislikes. And everyone had fun.

It is said that "shared laughter creates a bond of friendship." Never underestimate the power of a shared experience.

MAKING BEST USE OF ICEBREAKERS

Building Team

Icebreakers are an opportunity to build trust and a sense of team. They can help take our eyes off of ourselves and give everyone a common focus.

A short icebreaker can help your team to settle down and focus. And it's fine to mix it up a bit; have a fun icebreaker one session followed by a more meaningful or deep question the next time.

Relating the icebreaker to something relevant can help people to see the practical application in their own lives.

Introducing the Icebreaker

When introducing the activity, try not to use the word "icebreaker." Instead, say something like, "Jim's going to start us off this week. What have you got for us, Jim?"

It can help the flow if the person opening with the icebreaker can start with their own response to the question. This will give everyone an opportunity to consider their own response and make them feel more comfortable.

Icebreakers Are Inclusive

The icebreaker is something that even the newest person in your group can take part in, and even the quieter or more reticent can have an opportunity to share something.

Almost anyone can lead or come up with an idea for an icebreaker. Asking someone to open your time together by coming up with the icebreaker can be a great way to build confidence within the members of your small group. Don't forget to encourage individuals afterwards with a kind word, an email or a text message!

Involving Everyone

Encourage everyone to take part; simple questions such as, "What do you think, Nancy?" or, "John?" can persuade everyone to make their own small contributions.

If you are leading the group, be prepared to interrupt anyone who speaks too long or ventures way off topic.

Going Deeper

As your group grows and matures, you may find that the type of icebreaker you want to use or feel comfortable using may change.

As a general rule, an icebreaker should take no more than 10 to 15 minutes.

Finally, remember the golden rule of icebreakers:

"It's an icebreaker, not an <u>icemaker</u>!"

Laughter Is the Best Medicine

Try not to get too personal with questions. People who have been or are currently going through difficult times may find personal questions hard to answer without getting emotional. This is NOT the aim of this part of your time together.

Aim to have fun. Anything that gets people *laughing* builds real, closer bonds among the group.

ICE BREAKER 101 - TEN SIMPLE RULES

Icebreakers are simple, and they come with some simple rules to keep everyone in the group safe.

Here are 10 rules for successful icebreakers:

1. Keep it short
2. Make it fun
3. Keep it encouraging
4. Keep it upbeat
5. Keep it moving
6. Involve everyone
7. Keep it light
8. Encourage laughter
9. Keep it simple
10. Keep on doing it!

Of course, there will be times when you'll need to break these rules, but generally it is best to try to keep to them.

ICEBREAKER QUESTIONS

ABOUT YOU - FACTS & INFO

These are simple questions designed for people to get to know each other a little better and to get everyone to contribute. Many of the questions are factual so that even the shyest or most introverted person in your group can give an answer.

These easy icebreakers are aimed at newly formed groups and for meetings when newcomers are present.

- Are you a back seat driver?
- Do you like the mountains, plains or the coast? Why?
- What do you do to relax?
- How many different places or countries have you lived in?
- How many languages can you you speak?
- How many rings do you leave before you answer the phone?
- How many brothers & sisters do you have? Are you the oldest, a middle child, or youngest?
- If you were to perform in the circus, what act would you be?
- Are you a listener or talker?
- What's your favorite children's story?
- What music was playing in your car or iPod most recently?

- What compliment do people give you the most?

- What is currently set as the background on your computer?

- Tell us one thing you can do better than anyone else you know?

- What is the most interesting we may not know you?

- What is the name of the best movie you have ever seen & why?

- What is the title of the best book you have ever read & why?

- What is the strangest or unusual thing you've ever eaten?

- What is your favorite strange foods combination?

- What is your favorite way to waste time at work without getting caught?

- What is your occupation or hobby? What do you enjoy about it?

- What was the best movie that you have watched this month? This year?

- What's your middle name? Do you love or hate it?

- When was the last time you went to the movies & what movie did you see?

- When was the last time you went to the theatre & what did you see?

- Where did you grow up?   When did you last go back there?

- Where is the furthest you have travelled to?

- Who do you admire the most & why?

- Why do you live in this town or city?

• Would you rather be in a crowd, or be the last person left on earth?

FAVORITES -
HATES 'N' LOVES

Some of these are lighthearted, while others are a little more probing. They are useful to lighten the atmosphere, to add humor or to help the group discover more about each other.

- Are you a morning or night person?
- As a child, may favorite game was. . . . . .
- Describe your favorite pair of PJ's
- Do you like fruit? What's your favorite?
- Do you like vegetables? Which is your favorite?
- Do you prefer the pool or the beach?
- If you had to give up a prized possession, what would it be?
- What is your biggest pet peeve ?
- My favorite unusual food combination is .... and ....
- Name a favorite sound or noise, past or present and explain your choice
- Name one of your favorite things about someone in your family.
- Name one thing that you really couldn't live without
- Name your favorite song right now and your favorite song of all time?
- Name the one song that puts you in the Christmas spirit?

- Other than pizza, what is a favorite Italian dish?

- Tell us about your unusual hobby?

- What are your favorite hobbies?

- What are your favorite pizza toppings?

- What are your pet peeves or interesting things about you that you dislike?

- What are your favorite smells?

- What is your favorite cooking spice?

- What clubs where you involved in during High School, University or College?

- What did you eat for breakfast today?

- Name one thing that you have that is of sentimental value

- What is the best dessert you have ever had?

- What is your favorite "made up" word from your childhood or that of one of your children? Does it have a meaning?

- What is your favorite animal?

- What is your favorite breakfast?

- What is your favorite candy?

- What is your favorite cartoon character & why?

- What is your favorite color?

- What is your favorite TV commercial? Which commercial annoys you the most?

- What is your favorite Disney movie & what do you love about it?

- What is your favorite guilty pleasure?

- What is your favorite kind of pie? Describe taking a bite using three words to describe it.

- What is your favorite memory with someone other than family

- What is your favorite Christmas movie and why?

- What is your favorite movie of all time?

- What is your favorite number?

- What is your favorite pet's name?

- What is your favorite place to shop?

- What is your favorite quotation or poem?

- What is your favorite restaurant and why?

- What is your favorite season & why?

- What is your favorite scent, perfume or aftershave?

- What is your favorite soft drink?

- What is your favorite song to sing in the shower?

- What is your favorite flavor soup?

- What is your favorite sport? Which sports team do you support?   Rate your enthusiasm for your team from 1-10 (1=not interested, 10=crazy fan)

- What is your favorite table or board game?

- What is your favorite thing to do in the summer?

- What is your favorite activity in winter?

- What is your favorite tradition? (family tradition, church tradition, whatever)

- What is your favorite video game?

- What is your favorite winter activity?
- What is your favourite type of music/song etc?
- What is your most favorite pair of shoes ever & why?
- What is your very favorite part of your day?
- What kind of toothpaste do you use?
- What one food would you never eat?
- What song would you choose to sing for a karaoke evening & why?
- What was your favorite 80s movie?
- What was your favorite age and why?
- What was your favorite childhood toy?
- What was your favorite decade? (50's, 60's, 70's, 80's, 90's etc.) & why?
- What was your all-time favorite holiday?
- What was your favorite TV show when you were growing up?
- What was your favourite game when you were a kid?
- What's one of your favorite things to do when you have an evening off?
- What's the best dinner you have ever enjoyed?
- What's the most vintage piece of clothing you still own and wear?
- What's your favorite fabric and why?
- What's your favorite ice cream flavor?
- What's your favorite song to karaoke to?

- What's your favorite song to play at full volume & why?

- What's your favorite type of house? Describe it.

- What's your favorite line from a movie?

- What's your favorite way to celebrate an achievement?

- What's your favorite cartoon character, and why?

- What's your favorite thing to do in the summer?

- When you were in elementary or primary school, what was your favorite activity at recess or breaktime?

- When you were a child, who was your favorite super hero? Did you want to be like them?

- Who is your favorite movie star, and why?

- Who is your favourite relative & why?

- Who is your real-life hero? (this could be a family member, friend, a celebrity or unrecognised hero)

- Who was your favorite band, group, or solo artist when you were in high school?

- Who was your favorite teacher and why?

- Who was your favourite teacher at school - why?

- You are chosen to make dinner for a very special guest. What will you cook?

GETTING TO KNOW ONE ANOTHER - GOING DEEPER

Once everyone in your group has gotten to know each other a little better, these icebreakers are designed to help individuals know a bit about each other's likes, dislikes, personalities and backgrounds.

- Are you a patient or impatient driver?
- Are you a planner or a procrastinator? Can you give an example?
- Did you ever consider becoming a teacher? What would you teach?
- Did you have a nickname growing up or now? What was it and why were/are you called that?
- Do you eat everything put on your plate or do you always leave a little something?
- What's your attitude to money? Are you carefree or do you track every penny?
- What most annoys you about other people's attitude to money?
- How do you best like to spend your Saturdays? Sundays?
- How many car crashes/automobile accidents have you experienced?
- How many points do you currently have on your licence?

- Would the people who know you best say you are usually predictable or unpredictable? Give an example
- Would the people who know you best say you are well-organised or unorganised? Give an example
- Would the people who know you best say you are a practical person or impractical? Give an example
- Would the people who know you best say that you are patient or impatient? Give an example
- If we Googled your name what would we see?
- Is your glass half empty or half full?
- Name one life experience that helped make you who you are today?
- Name two things that this group doesn't know about you yet
- Tell us about a unique or quirky habit of yours
- What are you most talented at?
- What do you love most about living in this country?
- What famous person do you know or have met personally?
- What is one thing about you people would be surprised to learn?
- What is one thing you notice about people when you first meet them?
- What is the first thing you notice about the opposite sex?
- What is the longest book you have ever read?
- What is the most crazy thing you have done?
- What is your favorite animal & why?

- What is your favourite holiday spot and why do you enjoy it?

- What kind of music do you like?

- What magazine(s) do you subscribe to?

- What music track have you listened to most this week/month?

- What one question would you like to ask the person next to you?

- What one thing do you never eat when it's put in front of you?

- What person in the Bible do you most closely identify with?

- What thing makes you most happy & why?

- What three things do you believe without any doubts

- What TV advertisement annoys you the most?

- What was the last track or MP3 you downloaded?

- What was the most mischievous thing you did as a child?

- What was your first paid work?

- What's the best prize you've either won or almost won?

- What's the funniest thing you did as a kid that your parents still talk about to this day?

- What's your passion?

- What's the longest road trip you've ever made?

- When people look at me, what one thing would they never guess?

- When was the last time you did something for the first time? What was it?

- Which of the Simpson characters are you most like? What characteristics do you share?

- Who would you call to be bailed out of jail?

- Would you ever loan a large amount of money to a friend or relative ? Why or why not?

- Would you rather lead or follow? Why?

ABOUT FEELINGS -
UPS, DOWNS & EMOTIONS

Some of these questions encourage more intimacy than others, so remember to be sensitive to the needs and personalities of the people in your group.

A few of the icebreakers that discuss feelings may be more appropriate for women's groups than men's.

Choose wisely!

- Choose a word to describe a sunset!
- For what are you thankful?
- How do you express your anger ?
- How do you react when you aren't thanked for going out of your way for someone?
- How was school for you? What was the best thing about school?
- Is there anything would you like to change about your parents?
- What was your greatest disappointment?
- Name a turning point in your life that makes you smile
- Name a memorable moment in your life that makes you cry
- Standing alone & looking at stars, how does it make you feel or think?

- Tell us about a situation when you felt life had been unfair to you?

- Under what circumstances do you feel least lonely? Why?

- What are you thankful for?

- What do you love most? Why?

- What do you think is best feeling in the world?

- What do you think of when you think of tragedy? Why?

- What is one thing that still makes you feel guilty?

- What is your biggest fear or phobia?

- What is your most disappointing moment in life?

- What is your most embarrassing experience?

- What is your position in your family, oldest, middle, youngest? Who would you have liked to swap this position with?

- What one thing makes you laugh every time?

- What makes you feel the most secure?

- What one quality do you most value about one other person in the room?

- What scares you the most? What, if anything, can you do to help overcome your fears?

- What takes you out of your comfort zone?

- What was the last time you got really angry? What have you learnt about yourself?

- What was the scariest real nightmare you found yourself in?

- What world disasters has affected you most and why?

- When have you laughed the hardest recently?

- What was the last silly thing to make you cry?

- Which would you rather have a kiss or a hug? Why?

- Would you rather meet the love of your life, knowing he / she will die within a year, or go without meeting them? Explain your thinking.

ABOUT IDEAS -
CREATIVE THINKING

Some of these are thought-provoking and will require everyone to express an idea or opinion. You may find that men have an easier time talking about ideas than discussing their feelings.

These questions are designed to get people thinking on a deeper level and to share the things that make them tick.

- Describe one of the most beautiful things you have seen
- For what do you think you would be willing to lay down your life & why?
- Has a parent ever told you they were sorry or asked your forgiveness for something?
- Has any small group been a help to you? Why?
- Has modern technology enhanced or complicated your life? Why?
- If I asked your high school friends what they thought you would be doing today, what would they say?
- If someone bought you an island what would you do with it?
- If someone rented a billboard for you, what poster or sign would you put on it?
- If there was a whole different concept of reality (for example, The Matrix movie) how would you like it to look?

- Name someone you admire who has overcome considerable obstacles to get where they are now.

- What are your limitations and potentials?

- What book has influenced you greatly and how?

- What cartoon character best represents you?

- What do you look for in a friend?

- What do you think the best gift of the world is?

- What does "being real" mean to you?

- What institution is most in need of change? Why?

- What is the biggest waste you know of? Why?

- What is the greatest music ever composed?

- What is the hardest choice you have ever had to make? What was the outcome?

- What one modern convenience could you not live without?

- What one thing do you believe would make you the happiest person in the world if you had it?

- What stereotype do you think you might fit into?

- What was the most important decision is your life?

- What word best describes what you think about advertising?

- What would you do tomorrow if you weren't afraid?

- What's the most important thing to you in life?

- Name two historical figures you would invite to a dinner party

- Who has been the biggest inspiration to you and why?

- Who inspires you and in what ways are you similar?

- Who is the most interesting person you have met?

- You win a million dollars, but you have to give half to a charity. What charity would you pick and why?

- If this were your last day alive, what would you say to each person in the group?

- If you could change one thing about yourself what would you change? Why?

- What book would you write and why?

- What do you love most about Christmas-time?

- What do you think is the greatest invention in your lifetime and why?

- What is one lie you've told? What were the consequences?

- What are the greatest values that guide your life? Why?

- What is the most difficult choice you've had to make in your life up to this point? Who and what factors helped you make your choice?

- What is the most significant event in your life & why?

- What is your favorite way to express yourself and why?

- Which product would you refuse to promote if you were famous?

- What sound do you most associated with violence & why?

- What was the greatest peer pressure you felt as a teen? What is the greatest peer pressure you feel as an adult? How are you handling it'

- What's the kindest act you have ever seen?

- Which member of your family has had the greatest influence on your current way of thinking?

- Would you rather be rich or famous? Why?

- Would you rather be an undiscovered genius or famous, but mediocre?

- Would you rather be seven foot tall or four foot short?

- Would you rather live without the internet or your cell phone?

- Would you rather die in a plane crash, a sudden heart attack or be hit by a train? Why?

- Would you rather ride a motorbike across Russia or take a train trip across Europe?

- Would you rather die from too much heat or too much cold?

- Would you rather be immersed in a vat of cockroaches or snakes?

- Would you rather lose all your memories forever or lose all your hair?

- Would you rather have beautiful eyes or a fabulous body?

- Would you rather change a diaper or do the washing?

- Would you rather be a test pilot or a racing driver?

- Would you rather never listen to music or never read books?

About The Past - Looking Back, Learning & Understanding

Sometimes looking back at the past can help us understand ourselves and others more clearly.

This section is not appropriate for all groups. Be sensitive to the individuals in your group as you ask questions about the past.

- As a child, when you got caught doing something wrong, what were you most likely to do?

- Can you remember the registration number or number plate of your first car? What make and model was it?

- Have you ever gone back to the town where you grew up in? If yes, how has it changed? Is your old house still there?

- Have you ever had the police called at your home? What was the reason?

- Have you ever said something you initially regretted, but were eventually glad you said it?

- If given a chance to go back and change something that happened during the past, what would that time be and why?

- If you could live in any other time period of the past, what would it be and why?

- If your parents could have told you one thing as a teenager, what would you like to have heard?

- Share the biggest argument you had with your parents.

- Tell us something that most people in the group won't know about you.

- Andy Warhol stated that everyone gets 15 minutes of fame, what happened during your 15 minutes? Or what would you like to happen?

- What annoying line or phrase did your parents use over and over?

- What do you miss most about your childhood?

- What event in history are you most aware of as you plan your life? Why?

- What is a fashion trend that you used to wear (in the 70s, 80s, 90s, etc.) that you would now be too embarrassed to wear?

- What is the best thing you have done in your life?

- What is the longest road trip you've taken? Where was it to and how far was it?

- What is the funniest story your parents tell about you?

- What is one of the biggest regrets of your life?

- What is the most memorable event of your life and why?

- What is the scariest thing you have ever done for fun?

- What is your earliest memory from childhood?

- What is your favourite memory of Christmas?

- What is your favourite memory time spent, as a child, with one of your parents?

- What one rule did you always disagree with growing up?

- What superhero did you most want to be when you were a child?

- What time period from the past would you most have liked to live in and why?

- What was one of the most fun things you and your college friends did together?

- What was the best concert you went to? Who was it & when?

- What was the best year of your life? Explain why?

- What was the first live concert you ever attended?

- What was the first record or CD that you bought?

- What was the worst year of your life and why?

- What was your favorite childhood book?

- What's the hardest thing you've ever done?

- When did you last climb a tree?

- When you were 11, what did you want to be when you grew up?

- Where did you feel safest as a child?

- Which of your parents rules did you appreciate the most & why?

- Who is the most famous person you've ever met or seen?

- Who was your best friend as a young child? Do you still keep in touch with them today?

- Who was the object of your first big crush? Did they like you in return?

- Who was your hero when you were a child & why?

FUN ICEBREAKERS - DE-STRESS, UNWIND & RELAX

After a long or stressful day at work or at home, having some fun can help everyone unwind and relax.

Here are some fun, silly and downright impossible icebreakers to challenge and provoke your group!

• Are there any interesting things your name (first name or surname) spells with the letters rearranged?

• Describe a word beginning with the first letter of your name that sums you up?

• Do you have a birth mark? What, if anything, does it resemble?

• Do you make your bed every morning or do you leave it unmade?

• Do you prefer crunchy peanut butter or smooth?

• Do you prefer eating the frosting of the cupcake or the cupcake first?

• Do you prefer using a pen or pencil? Do you have a preference as to what make or brand?

• Do you squeeze the toothpaste from the top or the bottom?

• Do you tweet? Are you a Twitter fan? Rate yourself from 1-10 (1-novice, 10=addict)

• Have you ever been mistaken for someone famous?

- If someone made a movie of your life would it be a drama, a comedy, a romantic-comedy, action film, or science fiction? Why?
- If there was only one left of your favorite candy, who, if anyone, might you share it with?
- If you could be one color for the rest of your life, what color would it be & why?
- If you could chose to be an animal, what would you choose to be & why?
- If you could make your own 'sub' or sandwich - what fillings would you put in it?
- If you could spend your last hours of life with anyone, doing anything, who would you choose and what would you do?
- If you were a potato, what way would you like to be cooked?
- If you were decorating a chocolate cake, what would you use to decorate it?
- List five items everyone in the group has in common.
- Say one nice compliment about someone in this room.
- Tell two truths and one lie about yourself to the others in your group. Let the group try and guess which one is the lie.
- Which music CD would your friends be surprised to learn that you own?
- What do you most enjoy doing when you're at home?
- What would you like to do most with a free hour?
- What do you miss most about being a kid?
- What fantasy would you like to live out? Why?

- What gift would you most like to receive from others?

- What is one thing that always makes you laugh?

- What is something you have lost that you have never found, or were tremendously relieved when you did find it?

- What is the most embarrassing thing you have ever done?

- What is the craziest thing you've done lately?

- What is the most interesting class you've taken?

- What is the strangest gift you have ever received?

- What is your favorite pizza topping?

- What song most describes your life right now?

- What was the weirdest food you've ever eaten?

- What word would you add to the dictionary if you could & what would it mean?

- What would you rather wear, contacts or glasses?

- Which do you insist on, toilet paper rolled over or under?

- When are you at your silliest?

- What happened last time your power failed?

- When you are using the bathroom at someone else's home, what are you most likely to notice or comment on?

- When you were five years old, what did you want to be when you grew up?

- Which of Snow White's seven dwarfs describes you best and why? (Bashful, Doc, Dopey, Grumpy, Happy, Sleepy or Sneezy)?

- Which way do you eat corn on the cob?

- Who would you like to play your life story in a movie?

- Would you rather clean the house or play with the kids?

- Would you rather be really hot or really cold?

- Would you rather have a broken leg, broken nose or broken arm?

- Would you rather plan a party or attend one? Why?

- Would you live in space if you could never come back to earth?

- Would you rather go the short way slow, or take the long way fast if you got there in the same amount of time?

- You've just been hired to the design department of a cereal company. What toy or gimmick would you create or put in breakfast cereal box?

- You've just found out you have three months to live, who are the first three people you tell?

- You've just found out that you've won millions on the lottery, who would you share your winnings with?

HOPES & DREAMS - WISHES & DESIRES

Our hopes and aspirations tell a lot about us. They can help reveal our true desires and goals. Hearing others' hopes and dreams can help us see them in a different light too.

- "I wish everyone would "...................", complete the sentence
- Describe your dream wedding if money was no limit
- Have you ever had a recurring dream? What was it?
- If a movie was being made of your life and you could choose any movie star to play you, who would you choose and why?
- If there were a holiday in your honor what would it celebrate?
- If you knew that an atomic bomb were going to explode here in ten minutes time, what would you do?
- What would you do, if you knew you could not fail?
- If you where running for political office, what would your campaign slogan be?
- What are two of your goals for living?
- What future discovery would you love to see & why?
- What is the most dangerous/crazy/exciting thing you'd like to try? Why haven't you done it yet?
- What is your dream job?

- What one thing would you really like to see happen at the moment in your family? At work?
- What talent would you most like to grow & develop?
- What would you like to leave in your will for the person you care about the most?
- What would you like to be doing ten years from today?
- When do you sense being most alive? Why?
- Where would you like to retire and why?
- Why are you here?

ICEBREAKERS FOR WOMEN - LOVE, FEELINGS & MORE

Women often feel more comfortable when they have the opportunity to share their thoughts and feelings.

Here are some icebreaker questions that women may appreciate, though most are also appropriate for mixed groups.

• Choose one word to describe your life up to this moment?

• Describe your ideal romantic date?

• Did you ever go against a fashion trend? Why?

• Do you enjoy going shopping for clothes? Who is your best shopping companion?

• Do you love or loath ironing?

• How did you and your partner meet?

• How many children do you want? Girls or boys?

• How many pairs of shoes do you own?

• How much do you spend on hair or nails each month?

• If God would grant you any one request, what would it be?

• If you could have plastic surgery, what would you have done and why?

• If you were a lip gloss flavor, what would you be and why?

• What was a time in your life when you've felt jealous?

- What is one of the worst ways you've ever reacted to someone saying they loved you?

- Tell us about a day that you wanted to last forever

- What is greatest compliment you have ever received?

- Under what circumstances do you feel most or least lonely?

- What about your child (or children) makes you really angry?

- What article of clothing most closely describes your personality?

- What is something people can do to encourage you?

- Name one childish thing you still do as adult

- What could you do tomorrow to improve your life?

- What dessert describes you the best and why?

- What did you like best about your home?

- What do you feel is your most attractive physical feature?

- What do you feel that you need to make your life complete?

- What do you have in your bag or wallet that best describes your personality?

- What do you still want to accomplish with your life?

- What gift can you give others?

- What household chores do you hate the most?

- What is one thing about your day today that you haven't told anyone about?

- What is one thing that you constantly think about?

- What is the best reward anyone can give you?

- What is the first thing you think of when you wake in the morning?

- What is your best personal characteristic?

- What is your first thought in the morning?

- What kind of hat best describes your personality?

- What kind of footwear best describes you?

- What makes you cry and why?

- What one material thing or object have you thought about most this week?

- What qualities do you think are most important to encourage in children?

- What quality do you most value about your best friends?

- What question do you not like other people to ask you?

- What types of social situations make you most nervous?

- What specific thing have you done that impressed even yourself?

- What was the highest grocery bill you ever had this year?

- What was the title of the last self-help or inspiring book you read?

- When you do something stupid, how much does it bother you to have other people notice it?

- When's the last time you cried? Why?

- Who is your best friend? Tell us about them

- What do you remember about the first boy you fell in love with?

- You discover that the person you're in love with hates home cooking. What would you feed them?

ICEBREAKERS FOR MEN - SUCCESS, AMBITION, CARS & MORE

There is a great deal of pressure on men in our modern cultures. Some of these questions are experiential, while a few deal with thoughts and ideas.

These can help men in your group realize that they are not isolated in their thoughts and feelings as well as give them a common bond with others in the group.

- Describe an experience in your life that changed your values completely.
- Have you ever jumped out of a plane?
- If they made a movie of your life who would play you?
- If you could compete in the Olympics, what sport would you choose and why?
- If you were a UFC (Ultimate Fighting Champion) or wrestler, what would your name be?
- If you were to die tomorrow, what would your tombstone say?
- If your house were burning down, what would you take and why?
- Is it ever OK to waste time?
- What's the first thing you do when you wake up on Saturday morning?

- Name three things you think will become obsolete in ten years.
- Name all the vehicles you've owned in your life.
- Name one characteristic you look for in someone you consider a friend.
- Name three qualities you would look for in a potential partner?
- Tell us about one big problem you had to solve this year?
- Tell about the last time you had to ask someone for help?
- Tell us one of the worst fights you ever got into?
- Using just one word, name something significant about your life today.
- What are three things you would like to accomplish in the next year?
- What do people like best about you? Why?
- What did you learn from your last failure?
- What do you keep in the trunk of your car?
- What do you keep in your wallet apart from cards, money and photos?
- What do you spend most time worrying about?
- What household chore do you hate the most?
- What website do you surf to most often?
- What is in the trunk of your car right now?
- What is one of the books (other than the Bible) that has had the greatest influence on your life? Why

- What is the furthest you have travelled?

- What is the reason that you get up in the morning?

- What is the worst thing that you've done to attract attention?

- What mountain would you want to climb someday?

- What obstacles do you find when trying to become a close friend to someone of the opposite sex?

- What person has influenced your life the most? Why?

- What new or additional skill do you think you now need in order to succeed?

- What type of music do you listen to when you want to relax?

- What was the most embarrassing thing you have done while on a date?

- What are usually your last thoughts before going to sleep?

- What would you do if you had all the money in the world?

- What's the best sound effect you can make? How?

- What's more important to you, the journey or the destination?

- When was the last time you admitted you were wrong? Why is it so hard to do?

- What was the last time you cooked something? What did you cook?

- When was the last time you did something for the first time?

- When you lose electricity in a storm, do you light the candles or turn on the flashlight? How many of each do you own?

- When you were 6 years old, what did you want to be when you grew up?

- Which animal represents you the best and why?

- Would you rather be rich, or famous? Why?

- Would you rather live to be 100 and be sick, or live to be 50 and be healthy?

- Would you rather go whitewater rafting or hanggliding?

- You discover that the person you're in love with enjoys homemade desserts, what would you cook for them?

IF YOU COULD...
THINKING OUTSIDE THE BOX

Here are a few questions designed to get people thinking on their toes and out of their comfort zones. There are no right or wrong answers; the aim is to have fun and get a little creative.

- If you auditioned for a TV Talent Show, what song would you choose to sing and why?

- If you could give one sentence of advice to your younger self about how to live life well, what would it be?

- If you could ask God one question what would it be?

- If you could attend any college, free of charge, what college would that be and what subject would you study & why?

- If you could be a cocktail, what cocktail would you be and why?

- If you could be a cookie, what kind of cookie would you be?

- If you could be a film character, who would you be?

- If you could be a pair of jeans what style would you be? Why?

- If you could be a professional at any sport, what would it be?

- If you could be an ice cream or ice cream flavor, what would it be & why?

- If you could be any animal in the world, which animal would you be? Why?

- If you could be any color in the coloring box, what color would you be and why?

- If you could be any kitchen appliance, what would it be and why?

- If you could be any superhero, which one would you be and why?

- If you could be anything in the world, what would you be and why?

- If you could be anywhere, doing anything right now, where would you be and what would you be doing?

- If you could be in the Guiness Book of Records, what record-breaking feat would you attempt?

- If you could be in the Olympics, what skill or sport would you like to compete in?

- If you could be invisible for one day, what would you like to do and why?

- If you could be buried anywhere in the world, where would it be?

- If you could be one cartoon character who would you be and why?

- If you could bring one person back from the dead who would it be and why?

- If you could change one current event or news item in the world what would it be and why?

- If you could change one part of your body which part would it be & why?

- If you could change your diet, what would you change and why?

- If you could date any celebrity, who would it be and why?

- If you could drive / ride / fly anything to work, what would it be?

- If you could erase one day in history which one would it be?

- If you could fly or breathe under water which would you prefer?

- If you could fly to a different country, which one would you fly to??

- If you could go anywhere in the world, where would you travel?

- If you could go back and change your career what would you be doing now?

- If you could go only to one restaurant, which would you choose?

- If you could have an endless supply of one type of food, what would you choose and why?

- If you could have any kind of a job as an entertainer, what do you think you would do best?

- If you could have any super human power what would it be and why?

- If you could have one thing to drink before you died what would it be? and why?

- If you could go on tour with a celebrity or band, who would it be & why?

- If you could have written any book in history, what book would you like to have written?

- If you could become fluent in another language, what would that language be and why?

- If you could listen to only one music cd for the rest of your life, what would it be?

- If you could live anywhere for one year, all expenses paid, where would you live?

- If you could live in the city or the country, which would you choose & why?

- If you could meet any person from the Bible (other than Jesus) who would it be and what would you ask them?

- If you could mix several animals together, which parts of which animal would you choose to make the ultimate beast?

- If you could only take two things to a deserted island what would it be?

- If you could only take three people to an island from this group, whom will it be and why?

- If you could only where one color for the rest of your life, what would you choose and why?

- If you could own your own store, what would it be & why?

- If you could plan the ultimate vacation, where would you go and what would you do?

- If you could play any musical instrument, what would it be and why?

- If you could relive any part of your life, what would it be and why?

- If you could rid the world of one thing, what would it be?

- If you could be instantly transported somewhere else, where would you go?

- If you could switch your body with the body of a celebrity, who would you choose and why?

- If you could take back something you've once said to someone, what would it be?

- If you could talk to any one person now living, who would it be and why?

- If you ask three questions of any famous person from history, who would it be and what would you ask them?

- If you could time travel, where would you go, and who would you meet?

- If you could travel anywhere in the world, where would you go?

- If you could get a ticket to watch any sport in the Olympics, what sport would you choose and why?

- If you could visit any historic or heritage site in the world, where would you choose to go and why?

- If you could, would you become the President or Prime Minister? Why or why not?

- If you didn't have to worry about earning money what would you most like to do for the rest of your life?

- If you had a "theme song", what would it be?

- If you had a band, what would you name it?

- If you had a boat or yacht, what would you name it?

- If you had a magic lamp and a genie who granted you three wishes, what would the three wishes be?

- If you had one extra hour of free time a day, how would you like to use it?

- If you could play just one song at your wedding what would you choose and why?

- If you could choose between a bicycle, recreational vehicle, a sports car or an SUV, which would you choose and why?

- If you had the opportunity to live one year of your life over again, which year would you choose?

- If you had to be a flower, which one would you like to be and why?

- If you had to be handcuffed to one person for an entire month, who would you choose?

- If you had to choose between giving up your hearing or sight, which would you choose and why?

- If you had to describe your day (or week) as a traffic sign, what would it be?

- If you had to describe yourself using three words, what three words would you choose?

- If you had to enter a "Useless Talent" competition, what would talent would you enter?

- If you had to give up one food forever, what would it be?

- If you had to give up one modern convenience (e.g. computer, TV, computer, microwave, phone) what would it be & why?

- If you had to lose one of your five senses, which one of them would you prefer to lose and why?

- If you had to leave this country, what country would you move to? Why?

- If you had to paint the whole country only one color what would it be and why?

- If you had to wear the same design of t-shirt every day for the rest of your life, which word, image or phrase what would you choose?

- If you had unlimited money and space, which one thing would you buy for your home?

- If you had your own talk show, which three people would you invite to be your first guests & why?

- If you knew that tomorrow would be the last day of your life, how would you spend the day

- If you lost your sense of smell, what smell would you miss most?

- If you met your Maker tomorrow, what would you want Him to say and why?

- If you were a piece of fruit, what fruit would you choose to be?

- If you were a piece of furniture what would you be? Why?

- If you were a professional wrestler, what would your ring name be and why?

- If you were a spy what would your alias be?

- If you were a super hero what would your special power be and why?

- If you were a tree, what kind of tree would you be and why?

- If you were an animal, what would you be and why?

- If you were attending a costume party, what would your costume be and why?

- If you were blind for the rest of your life, what would you miss seeing the most?

- If you were elected mayor, what would be your first change and why?

- If you were offered free skydiving lessons would you accept them? Why or why not?

- If you were God, what one thing would you do today?

- If you were in the "Miss/ `Mr. America" talent competition, what would you choose as your talent?

- If you were on death row, what would you choose to eat for your last meal?

- If you were on the cover of a magazine, which one would it be?

- If you were stranded on a desert island, what three books would you take with you? Why?

- If you were to be on a reality TV show which one would you be on and why?

- If you were to die tomorrow, what would you like your tombstone to say?

- If you wrote a book about yourself, what story would it tell?

- If your house was on fire, what one thing would you take and why?

- If your plane was about to crash, who would you want sitting next to you?

QUESTIONS OF FAITH - EXPLORING BELIEFS

A well-chosen icebreaker can encourage people to reflect and open up, even in the first few minutes of your small group meeting. These questions are aimed at faith-based groups such as churches and cell groups.

Don't leave choosing an icebreaker until the last minute; instead, give it the same priority as you would any other part of the meeting.

- Do you know anyone who's seen an angel? Tell us about it.

- Have you ever seen God heal anyone? When & how?

- If you could ask God one question, what would it be? What was the last thing you saw God do?

- Share the most meaningful verses from a Holy book (e.g. the Bible) to you and why they are so meaningful?

- What book has most helped you in your journey of faith?

- What do you value most in a human relationship? In God? Your parents?

- What have you learned recently from a man or woman of faith?

- What inspiring story has most helped you?

- What is something unexpected that has changed about you in the last few years?

- What is the best thing that has ever happened in this group?

- What is the one thing you would like to ask God?

- What is the most outrageous thing you've done for God?

- What one characteristic of God are you most thankful for?

- When has God most surprised you?

- When you meet God, what would you hope He will say to you?

- Which Bible character do you most identify with and why?

THE PAST WEEK -
SHARING PERSONAL HIGHS AND LOWS

Small groups can focus on many things, but day-to-day life sometimes gets lost. These icebreakers focus on recent events or the past week to help individuals honestly share their high and low points.

• Describe your past week in the words of a weather forecast

• Describe one thing which has stressed you out this week?

• Tell us about the coolest or strangest thing that has happened to you this week?

• What thought has been constantly in your mind this week?

• What encouraging action have you taken this week?

• What has brought you most joy in the past week?

• What has happened to you during this week which you would like to tell the rest of the group

• What is the biggest challenge you have overcome in the past week?

• What is the one thing you want to accomplish next week?

• What is your concept of a fruitful day?

• What items of news has been most on your mind this week and why?

- What was the most important event during the past week?

- Who has had the greatest influence on your life since we last gathered?

THE WORST ....
EXPLORING AND REFLECTING

Here are a few fun ideas as well as some more reflective questions. Some of these may only be appropriate for groups whose members know each other well and have built a sense of trust between them.

- Describe your worst day ever

- Name the worst movie of all time

- What is the first lie you ever told?

- What is the best or worst pick up line you have ever heard or used?

- What is the worst name you've heard people call a child?

- What is your worst nightmare?

- What is your worst personality characteristic?

- What was your worst or best experience at summer camp?

- What was the worst advice you ever gave?

- What was the worst concert you went to (who and when)?

- What was the worst punishment your parents ever gave you?

- What was the worst smell you have ever smelled?

- What was your worst summer or part-time job?

- What were your best/worst subjects in school and what subjects would you want to learn now?

- What's the worst trouble you got into when you were young? What did you do?

- When was your most recent or dramatic car trouble?

TEAM BUILDING GAMES & ACTIVITIES - BUILDING TRUST

Although termed "games," these are more like activities that help individuals take the focus off of themselves and feel more at ease with each other.

Whether it's a new group or an existing group, games can be helpful as icebreakers, warm-ups or energizers.

For new groups, this can help build trust and openness between individuals and as a group. Though some people may feel that these are superficial, the bonding that happens as you share and take part over time is very real.

You can modify or adapt most of these games to suit the size and composition of your group. As your group works together, you'll notice leaders emerging. This can be helpful in developing their gifts as leaders and helping them to realize that people are following their lead.

Consider whether there are genuine activities within your organization or church that your group can undertake together to help build and develop a sense of team. For example, you could try working together to do gardening or painting for a vulnerable member of the community.

Whatever activity or game you choose, be aware of the risks. You may need to help people deal with conflicts, overcome fears and ensure that everyone gets involved.

Over the next few pages, we outline over twenty of our own personal favorite teambuilding games and activities that we've found to be fun, enjoyable and effective.

Birthday Game

This is a good get-to-know you game for a group of any age. The aim is to arrange everyone in a line in order of their date of birth.You can either choose to order by month or year of birth.

The catch is that no talking is permitted, everything has to be done visually and in silence.

Blindfold Game

This is a game to help build good communication. For each team you'll need a blindfold, a paperclip and good size room.

Blindfold one team member and then place the paperclip on the floor approximately 5-15 metres away from them. Their team mates then need to direct them using simple instructions, for example, right, left, stop, down, forward, etc.

Empires

This is great fun as a team or party game.

Each person has to think of someone well known or famous that everyone is the room is likely to have heard, they may be alive, dead or imaginary (e.g. Marilyn

Monroe, Father Christmas or the President of America) that they want to be for the game.

Someone is assigned the role of Empire Manager and asked to leave the room with a pen and paper. Each person has to leave the room and tell the Empire Manager, in secret, what their name is. The Empire Manager writes each name down, but in random order.

Once everyone has given their names to the Empire Manager, the Manager returns to the room and slowly and deliberately reads out each name on the list. For groups playing this for the first time, or large groups with more than 10 people, it may be helpful to read the names out twice.

The person sitting to the right of the Empire Manager starts the game by choosing one individual and asking them if they are one of the names read out (e.g. Jane, are you Marilyn Monroe?). If they guess correctly, Jane then comes and joins that person's empire. If they guess incorrectly, then Jane can choose another individual and ask if they are one of the names read out. You may not ask the same name as the person before you.

The winner is the person with the largest team when the final name is guessed.

The team part really comes into it's own for larger groups when remembering all the names that were read out can be quite a feat!

Egg Car

This is an opportunity for teams to get creative.

Tell each team (of 2-5 people) that they work in an automobile company and have been given the task of making cars safer. They need to design a vehicle that will prevent the passenger (in this case, an egg) from being injured.

Supply each team with a box of 6 eggs, and a range of materials, including some of:- balloons, bubble wrap, cotton wool, elastic bands, sponge, springs. Have one test ramp that they can use. with a hard surface at the lower end (e.g. wall).

Each team needs to brain storm ways to build a "car" that will protect the passenger (the egg) as they hit the wall at the end of the ramp.

The winning teams are those whose eggs survive impact.

Freeze Tig

This popular game has several names, including "Stuck in the Mud". This is very popular with children and younger people and best played in a large room or outside.

Select one person to be "it", this person then tries to catch and tag other individuals. When the person is "tagged" they must stand still where they are caught. Free players can "unstick" stuck players by tapping them on the shoulders and shouting "free".

Human Bingo

This game enables the group to find out more about each individual in the group, as well as encouraging them to ask questions of each other.

If you have time beforehand, ask everyone in the group to give you three achievements, sports, or other interesting things that other may not know about them. For example, "Played for England", "Written a Book", "Climbed Mount Everest", as well as more modest achievements such as "played rugby", "been white water rafting" etc.

Using a spreadsheet, create a simple bingo card, writing one achievement, hobby or sport in each square. Print off sufficient copies for everyone in the group.

Each person has to find at least one person who matches each square i.e. has played rugby, been white water rafting, etc (in our example, above). This is a great opportunity to get to know each other but also to have other conversations based around these interests and can also help individuals discover shared interests and experiences.

Invisible ball

If you're looking for something to bring out the creativity in your group, this activity is ideal.

Ask the group to form a circle. Start bouncing a ball and then throwing it to individuals, asking them to throw it back to you. After this short warm-up, it's time to get creative!

Put the ball away and tell the group that they're going to be playing with a range of balls, in a variety of sizes and types.

Start to bounce your invisible ball, then explain that you're going to throw it someone, calling out their name and telling them what type of ball it is (e.g. Martin, tennis ball). Then throw it to them, they now need to do the same, only calling out another name, and changing the type of ball.

If people don't know other's names, they can look at someone and ask their name, making this a good game for acquaintances to get to know each others names well.

When it's time to end the game, you can simply ask them to throw the ball back to you. A more fun way to end is to ask them to find a creative way to end the game.

Machine Game

This is great if you have plenty of people and can break into several groups of 5-8 people.

Ask each group to become a machine - they have to determine what the machine for and then each individual has to play a part in the machine.

Allow them 5-10 minutes of "rehearsal" time before they come back together, explain and demonstrate their "machine".

Map Game

Break into teams of 4-6 individuals.

Give each team a map, sheets of paper and a pen.

Tell the teams that their task is to plan a vacation for the team. Tell them how much they have to spend and any other restrictions. Set a time limit.

At the end of the time limit, each team feeds back the vacation the chose to plan and explains the reasons for their choices.

Memory Game

Find 30-40 household items and place 15-20 items on two trays.

Bring the first tray into the room and allow 2 minutes for individuals to observe it's contents. Then remove the tray and ask each individual to write down as many of the items as they can remember. Allow no more than 5 minutes for them to write these down. Get people to score how many they remembered correctly and make a note of their answers.

To develop this game further, split the group into teams of 2 or 3. Carry out the same exercise with the 2nd tray of objects, but allowing the teams to work together on remembering. Do everything exactly the same as before. Compare how many items each team remembered.

In most cases, the teams will remember far more than individuals working together, thus giving a very practical demonstration of working together as a team.

Orienteering

Split into teams of 2 or 3. Each team must navigate to points on a map. This could be something as simple as a map of your building or a few streets in your neighbourhood. At each point there must be something they need to note - a number, name - and return with all answers completed. Set teams off 5 minutes apart and time their return arrival, the winning team is the team to complete all answers correctly and take the shortest time.

Problem Solving

There are many problem-solving games, but here's a fun one that will test people's skills and ingenuity. It also demonstrates how important it is that each person works effectively and well in their own area, showing how effective the working of the team can be.

Take a photograph or image of a popular person or location. Cut into equal size squares - allowing one square for each member of the group.

Give each person a square of paper that is 4-6 times as large as the original square and ask each person to copy out the key part of their square on to the paper.

Once everyone has finished, the task is to reassemble all the hand-drawn pieces into one massive image.

Quiz/Trivia

An opportunity for some members of the group to shine and to build communication skills (and patience)!

Write or download a quiz of between 20-50 questions. You may choose to give 1 point for each question, or give 2 or 3 points for the more complicated questions.

Break into teams of 3-5. Give each team an answer sheet and pen. Ask each team to give themselves a team name (e.g. The Brilliant Bruisers, The Genius Giants).

As you read out the quiz questions, get each team to choose and write their answer on the answer sheet. Once all the questions have been read out, give the team a minute or so to complete any unanswered questions.

Now ask the teams to pass their answer sheet for marking to the team on the right/clockwise direction from themselves. Thus each team is marking another teams paper. Go through the correct answers, with each team marking the others paper.

At the end, add up all the points for the team and hand the paper back.

The winners are the team with the most points.

This is one occasion where a small prize (e.g. candy to share) goes down very well with the winning team.

Scavenger Hunt

Break into groups of 3-4 individuals.

Give each group a list of 10-15 items that they need to find (for example, safety pin, pen, CD, chewing gun, memory stick).

This could be as simple as a list of things that are in the room, or could include things you could find within a 5 minute walk of where you are meeting (e.g. leaf, flower, etc). The first team to come back with every item on the list is the winner.

Sheet of Paper Game

Break into small groups of 2 or 3 individuals. Each team is given several A4 or Foolscap sheets of paper (or sheets of newspaper) and a pair of scissors.

Each team has to solve the problem of how to cut the paper in such a way that they will be able to step through it. Setting a time limit can help teams speed up and try a variety of solutions quickly.

The winners are all the teams that manage to step through the piece of paper successfully within the time limit.

You can find a diagram of the solution to this problem at http://www.businessballs.com/freeteambuildingactivities.htm

Similarities

The aim is to get each individual to talk with every other person in the room.

Ask each person to find something new in common with each person in the room - for example "love ice skating", "hate peanut butter", "have two brothers", pretty much anything goes. This is a great way to get people talking and sharing, as well as realising how much they share with the other people in the room.

Surroundings

This is a fun exercise to help energise your group and see how much they notice about their surroundings.

Write a list of 10-20 questions about the building, home or venue that you are in. For example, building/door number, door color, floor color, etc.

Get teams of 2-5 to take your questions and work on answering them together. This can be particularly amusing if you meet in the same place week after week.

The winner is the team who answers the most questions correctly.

Trust Fall

This is aimed more at groups that already know each other and is aimed at building trust between individuals.

There are two versions of the Trust Fall that work for small groups. The first is where one person is caught by two individuals, crossing their arms in front of their chest, and falling gently towards the individuals who catch them.

The other is to have a tight circle of individuals, with one person at the centre who is blindfolded, and asked to fall and trust that they will be caught.

Clearly there is some risk to this game, so it is up to the person running the game to ensure the safety of all participants.

Truth & Lie

This is a party game that's a little similar to poker, in that it's all about bluffing your opponents.

Take turns for each person in the room to tell two truths and one lie about themselves. Give everyone a few seconds or up to a minute to consider which is likely to be the lie. Go around the room with each person saying which statement they believe is a lie (and why, if they wish). At the end, the individual declares which statement is a lie. Everyone who guessed that it was a lie gets a point. For every person who guessed incorrectly, the individual who told the lie gets a point.

The winner is the person with most points after everyone has taken a turn.

Tug of War

This is a popular game in the forces, helping individuals to fully understand that the strength is in the team, not in the strength of one individual.

Form the group into two teams. A rope is marked with a centre line and two markers 4m either side of the centre line. The teams start with the rope's centre line directly above a line marked on the ground, and once the contest (the "pull") has commenced, attempt to pull the other team such that the marking on the rope closest to their opponent crosses the centre line.

It's best to play this as the best of three goes, so that your teams can begin to understand where best to place the stronger and weaker members of the team.

Who Am I?

A simple five minute warm-up game that's easy to organise. Before the group arrives, prepare by writing the names of famous people on a number of post-its or labels. As each person arrives place the post-it or label on their back, where they can't see or touch it, but where others can clearly see it.

The aim of the game is to ask questions of others in the room to find out who you are. To find out more about them, and to guess who they are, individuals need to talk with others in the room and ask simple questions to which the answer can only be "Yes" or "No". Example questions are "Am I alive?", "Am I female?", "Am I famous?".

The game ends when everyone has found out who they are.

Witty Captions

This encourages working together and the involvement of each individual for a team result. Divide the group into teams of 2 or 3.

Cut out and give each team photographs from this week's newspapers. Ask each team to write an appropriate, witty or humorous caption for each photograph. After 10 minutes share your work with the group.

CONCLUSION - BUILD YOUR TEAM!

After seeing this range of icebreakers, I hope that you've seen the value of using them with your group.

In the same way that serving refreshments is an integral part of many church meetings, the icebreaker serves a key purpose and should be valued and enjoyed.

What's the most interesting "Ice Breaker" Question you have ever been asked? Email us at ice@hopebooks.org with your suggestions, and we'll include the best suggestions in the next edition of this book.

ACKNOWLEDGEMENTS

We would like to offer our thanks to the following individuals and organizations who allowed us to include their icebreakers, games and activities in this book.

Without them, the book would have been a lot leaner – we'd certainly never have come up with 600 icebreaker questions on our own!

Thanks to:

- Chris Hall

- Jerry Hampton

-Kenny Graiven

-and others, you know who you are

ABOUT THE AUTHOR

Jennifer has been writing and publishing since 2004.

She has written a number of Christian titles which have been published, including a daily devotional, "Daily Readings for Difficult Days."

Jennifer has three grown children and one granddaughter. She lives in Wiltshire, close to the cathedral city of Salisbury.

You can find her latest books & devotionals at

http://www.hopebooks.org.

Jennifer's blog is at http://www.hopeunlimited.co